Contents

Introduction

Fall holds warm memories from my childhood that have continued throughout adulthood. With these memories inevitably come the classic Halloween monsters we all recognize—vampire, witch, mummy, and Frankenstein. I designed each piece in this booklet using a carving-on-the-corner approach, which allows the carver to achieve added depth and interest without wasting a ton of wood. Take your time, relax, and carve away. Before you know it, these guys will have taken over your shop space and—just maybe—the hearts of your friends and family. Happy Halloween!

Count Dracula

Hone your carving and painting skills on this toothy troublemaker

As a child, I would often plan a Halloween costume for weeks in advance, and for many years Dracula was my character of choice. I'd read volumes and volumes on the lore behind this fascinating (and fearsome) character! Now, as an adult, I still have a soft spot for the Count—and when the cooler weather hits, he becomes a carving staple for me once again.

Getting Started

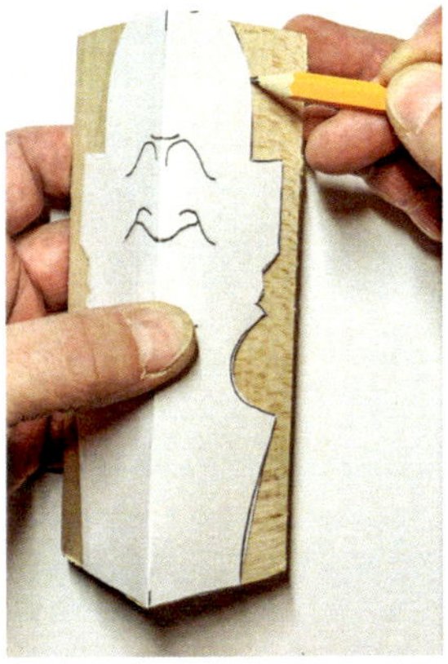

Cut your blank vertically in half from corner to corner; use a band saw. This will result in two long triangles, one of which you can save for a future project. Photocopy the pattern, cut it out, and fold down the centerline. Trace the pattern onto one of the blanks, making sure the grain runs vertically from head to chest. (This gives more support to delicate areas, such as the nose.) The center of Dracula's face will correspond exactly with the corner of your blank. Cut around the perimeter of the pattern with a band saw; I use a ¼" (6mm)-wide blade with 6 teeth-per-inch (TPI). If you don't have a band saw, you can use a coping saw or scroll saw. Save the paper pattern for future use.

Make sure all your tools are sharp, and periodically stretch your hands and wrists while carving.

ROUGHING OUT

1 **Mark the nose and chin.** Holding the pattern over the surface of the blank, cut small triangles under the nose and chin, and mark the lines with a pencil.

2 **Make a stop cut under the chin.** Use a knife. Remove the chip from the neck and chest area. Make a stop cut below the nose and carve up to it to form the mouth and chin area. Then determine how big you'd like the nose to be and where the hair will lie. Use the same stop and relief cuts to establish what will later be the eye sockets and bottom of Dracula's widow's peak.

3 **Draw the reference lines around the face.** Include the centerlines, hair, nose, and smile lines. Then carve along the pencil lines with a ½" (13mm) 90° V-tool. I use the larger V-tool on its side to shape the face and forehead instead of switching back and forth between tools. Make deep cuts along the hairline to separate the hair from the forehead; if you need to make several passes, that's okay. Shape the ears to give them a flat, pointed look; use the same tool. Make sure all cuts near the nose are angled away from the tip and not straight in; otherwise, you will snap the nose off. *Note: When making cuts, carve upward in the areas above the eyes and downward in the areas below.*

4 **Plot the details.** Draw reference lines for the upper brow, upper eye area, teeth, and clothing with a pencil. Redraw the centerline.

5 **Define the eyebrows.** Carve grooves above the brow line and upper eyelid area with a ¼" (6mm) #9 gouge. Make sure that you carve the inside (nose side) deeper so the grooves aren't the same depth across. Add nostril holes, pushing them straight into the sides of the carving and not upward into the nose. Clean up all cuts with a knife.

ADDING DETAILS

6 **Separate the teeth.** Then separate the collar from the coat. Use a ¼" (6mm) 45° V-tool turned on its side.

TIP

USE A V-TOOL TO GIVE CLOTHES CHARACTER

Want to add interest to a carved piece of clothing? Learn to use the V-tool on its side. This establishes large, flat planes to catch the light and creates a more distinct separation between "overlapping" layers, such as Dracula's coat and collar. You'll also save time by not having to go back and remove wood with a knife.

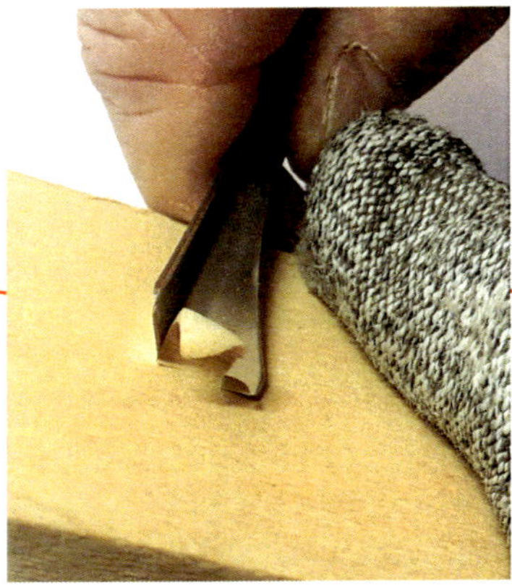

7 **Add shadow and depth to the smile.** Use the knife to cut a triangle on either side of the mouth.

8 **Shape the hair.** Use the knife to add waves and movement as desired. Remove all hard lines from the carving, and round and soften the forehead and nose.

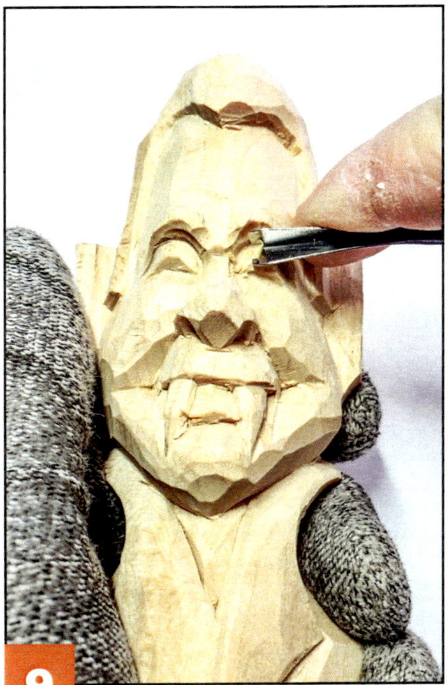

9 **Cut the upper eyelid crease.** Use the ¼" (6mm) 45° V-tool. Angle the V-tool upward, away from the eye, and cut deeper into the wood on the nose side, rounding the eyes.

10 **Redraw the eye lines, if desired.** Then rough in the exposed eyeball; use the same tool.

11 **Gently shape the eyes.** Use the knife. You want a nice, round area to paint, not a flat, football shape. Remove a small amount of wood at a time.

12 **Carve the eye bags.** Use the ¼" (6mm) 45° V-tool. Then detail the ears, following the ear angles straight in to refine their points. Cut in to add a slight ridge on the upper part of each ear, running in from the point to the hair.

13 **Add the final details.** Make a line around the collar area and refine the teeth; use a ⅛" (3mm) 45° V-tool. Clean up all remaining chips and fuzzies with the knife. Then add some stop cuts around the clothing areas to keep the paint from running later.

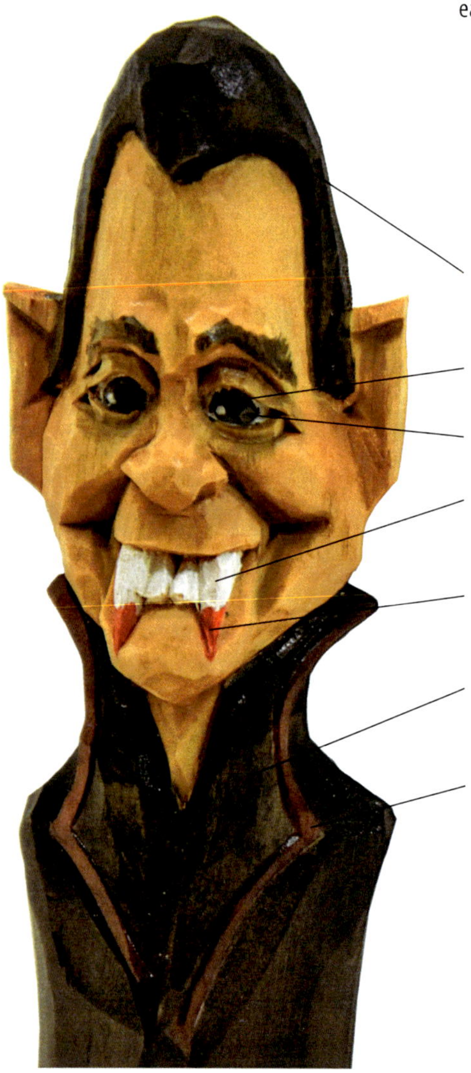

Paint Notes

Hair, eyebrows: 1 drop black (1), 1 drop water

Pupil: unthinned black (1)

Iris: unthinned grey (1)

Teeth, white in eyes, reflection in iris: unthinned white (1)

Bloodstains: unthinned bright red (1)

Cloak: 2 drops metallic black (2), 2 drops water

Cloak trim: 1 drop cloak mixture, 1 drop bright red (1)

Shadows: 1 drop midnight blue (2), 9 drops water

1 Plaid Apple Barrel
2 FolkArt

Painting and Finishing

Cover the flesh areas with a light water-based stain diluted with water to 50%. I use Minwax with a honeycomb tint. Then paint the eyes, teeth, cloak, and cloak trim. If desired, use a hair dryer between colors to speed up the drying time. Add the irises, pupils, and shine to the eyes, and then move on to the hair, brows, and bloodstains. After the paint is dry, brush midnight blue thinned to a 10% dilution into the shadows in the eyes, ears, and smile lines; this will give Dracula a grim, ghostly feel.

After everything is dry, brush on boiled linseed oil and let dry for three to four days. Finish as desired; I brushed on a water-based polyurethane.

Dracula Patterns

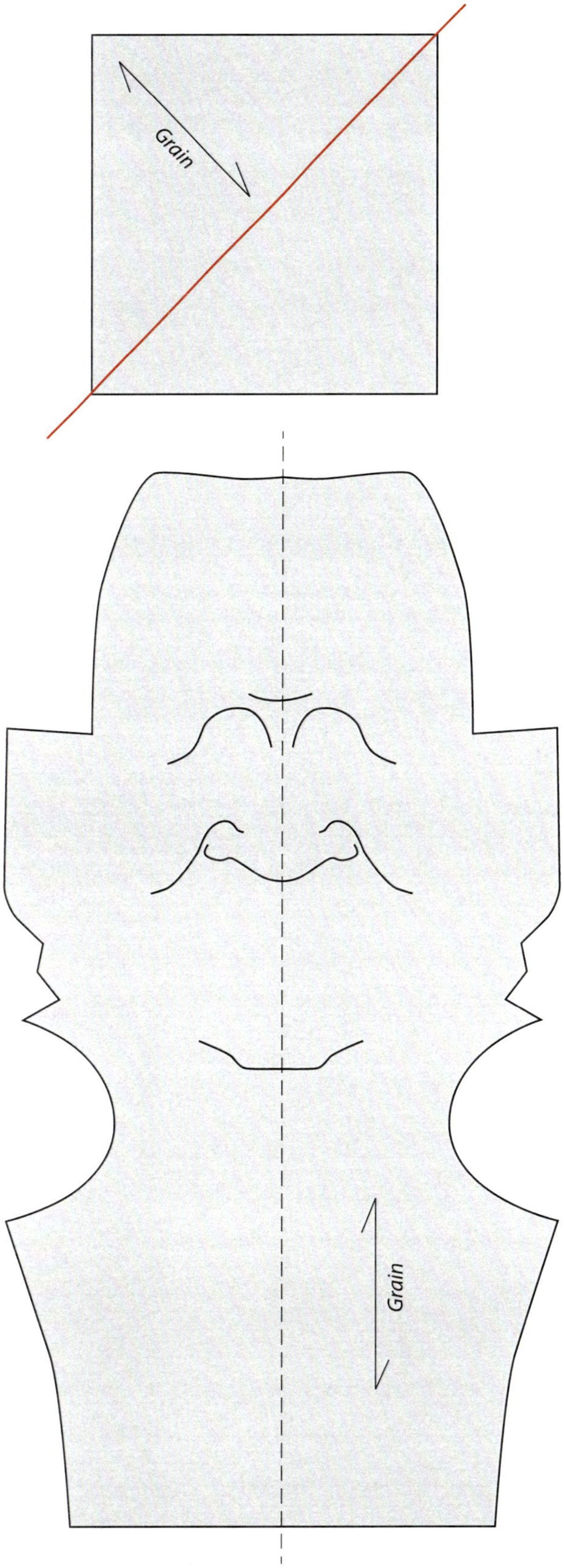

materials & **tools**

MATERIALS

- Basswood, 2" (5.1cm) square: 6" (15.2cm), cut vertically in half
- Pencil or marker
- Acrylic paints, such as Plaid Apple Barrel: black, bright red, grey, white; such as FolkArt: metallic black, midnight blue
- Water-based stain, such as Minwax: tinted honeycomb
- Boiled linseed oil
- Water-based polyurethane, such as Deft

TOOLS

- Band saw with blade: ¼" (6mm) wide
- Knife
- V-tools, 45°: ⅛" (3mm), ¼" (6mm)
- V-tool, 90°: ½" (13mm)
- #9 gouge: ¼" (6mm)
- Paintbrush
- Hair dryer (optional)

The author used these products for the project. Substitute your choice of brands, tools, and materials as desired.

CARVING A Witch

This cackling character will delight you—and your little dog, too

Witches have a somewhat mixed reputation. From *The Wizard of Oz* to *Snow White* to Shakespeare's *Macbeth*, they've hijacked the spotlight (and our secret admiration) in many a tale, armed with vim, mystery, and a whole lot of warts. If it's your first time carving a classic witch, that needn't spell disaster—with my easy-to-follow steps, you'll be making your friends green with envy in no time.

Getting Started

Cut your blank vertically in half from corner to corner; use a band saw. This will result in two triangles, one of which you can save for a future project. Photocopy the pattern, cut it out, and fold down the centerline. Trace the pattern onto one of the blanks, making sure the grain runs vertically from head to chest. (This gives more support to delicate areas, such as the nose and chin.) Cut around the perimeter of the pattern with a band saw; I use a ¼" (6mm)-wide blade with 6 teeth-per-inch (TPI). If you don't have a band saw, you can use a coping saw or scroll saw. Save the paper pattern for future use.

Make sure all your tools are sharp, and periodically stretch your hands and wrists while carving.

ROUGHING OUT

1 Make V-cuts to mark the main landmarks. Use a knife.

2 Draw in the reference lines. Do this for the hat rim, bottom of nose, bottom of chin, and bottom of collar. These will follow the V-cuts you just made. Notice how the cuts line up with the existing ones on each side of the blank. With a ½" (13mm) 90° V-tool, cut the lines you just drew. Try to accomplish each cut in a single pass.

3 Establish the brow area. With the carving knife, cut just below the bottom of the hat rim down toward the nose. Then remove the chip by cutting from the tip of the nose upward toward the rim of the hat. Make similar chips on either side of the nose to create the basic shape.

4 Shape the hat. Cut from the top of the hat (just below the point) downward toward the hat rim; use the knife. You are carving with the grain, so cut carefully, as extra force can cause the wood to split. Round the top of the hat slightly with a relief cut. Then round the entire hat, including the back, which begins at the level of the top of the hat brim in front.

5 Shape each side of the face. Use the ½" (13mm) 90° V-tool. The goal is to continue the cut deeper toward the back of the carving. Leave around ¼" (6mm) of thickness from the back of the blank and on either side, so you'll have room to carve the hair.

6 Separate the eyebrows and create the smile lines. Use the ½" (13mm) 90° V-tool; this ensures that both sides are even.

7 **Mark the spaces for the eyes.** With the knife, cut a triangle into each eye socket just below the brow line, following the same contour as the top of the brow line you created earlier.

8 **Carve the basic shape of the eye.** Use a ⅛" (3mm) 45° V-tool. Carve the top cut upward and the bottom cut downward.

ADDING DETAILS

9 **Remove a triangle on either side of the eye.** Use a detail knife. Be sure to angle the cuts, rather than stabbing them straight into the eye. Carve under the hat rim to clean up and separate the two areas. Use the same tool.

10 **Carve the mouth.** Use a ¼" (6mm) 45° V-tool. Try to keep the line somewhat flat to give the witch a bit of a sneer.

11 **Add a wart on her chin.** Use the knife. It doesn't need to be symmetrical—the uglier the better. Shape the chin down a bit to make the wart stand proud.

12 **Add the bottom lip and nose holes.** Use a ¼" (6mm) #9 gouge. Remove the nose hole chips with the detail knife.

13 **Shape the bottom of the collar.** Use the ¼" (6mm) #9 gouge. Notice that the tool is upside down. *Note: I don't measure the spacing—I just eyeball it.* Then turn the tool right-side up and carve the top of the collar between the bottom cuts. This creates a wavy movement in the fabric.

14 **Remove the chips on the collar.** Use the ¼" (6mm) #9 gouge. Clean up the collar area with the knife.

15 **Establish the amulet.** Use a ⅜" (10mm) #9 gouge. Make the cut by pushing the gouge into the wood, removing it, turning the tool, and pushing it back in to complete the circle. Do not turn the tool while it is in the wood, as this will break the wood fibers. Relieve the area around the amulet with the knife.

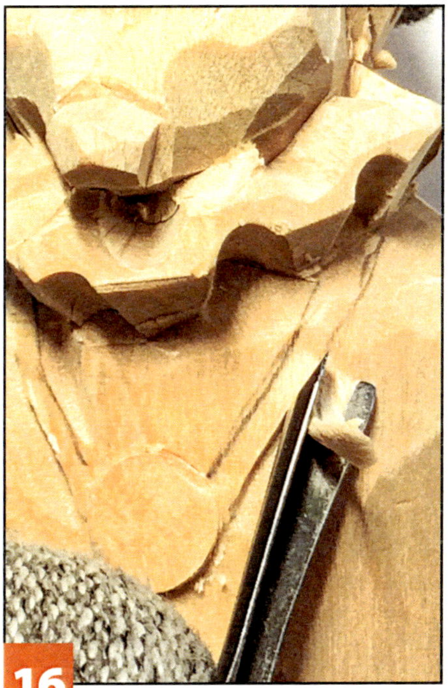

16 **Carve the amulet chain.** Use the ¼" (6mm) 45° V-tool. Lay the V-tool on its side, using it like a chisel. (See the tip on page 5.) This creates layers easily. Then clean up any chips, hidden fuzzies, high spots, and pencil marks on the carving. Use the knife. Add some stop cuts around the clothing areas to keep the paint from running later.

Paint List

White in eyes: unthinned white

Iris: unthinned Christmas green

Pupil: unthinned black

Flesh: 2 drops Christmas green, 3 drops water

Clothing: 2 drops purple, 2 drops water

Amulet chain, hair: 1 drop black, 1 drop water

Amulet: unthinned cardinal crimson

Acrylic paints: Plaid Apple Barrel

Painting and Finishing

Paint the eyes, skin, and clothing. If desired, use a hair dryer between colors to speed up the drying time. Add the irises, pupils, and shine to the eyes, and then move on to the hair, brows, and amulet.

After everything is dry, brush on boiled linseed oil and let dry for three to four days. Finish as desired; I brushed on a water-based polyurethane.

Witch Patterns

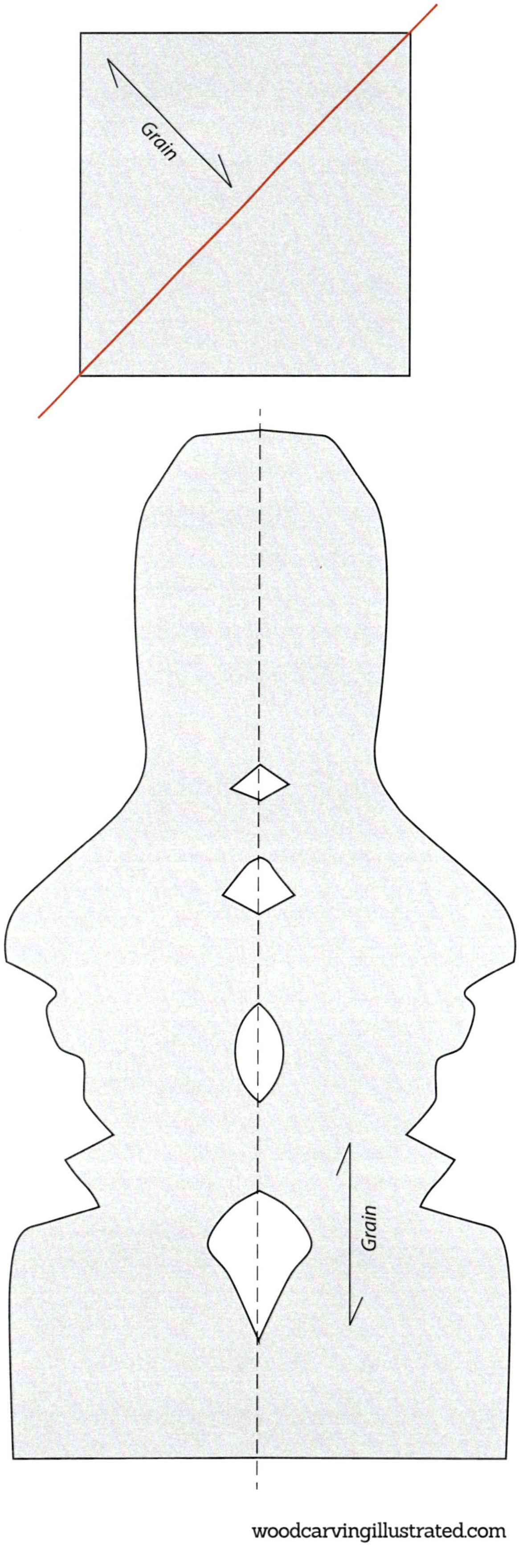

materials & tools

MATERIALS

- Basswood, 2" (5.1cm) square: 6" (15.2cm), cut vertically in half
- Pencil or marker
- Acrylic paints, such as Plaid Apple Barrel: black, cardinal crimson, Christmas green, purple, white
- Boiled linseed oil
- Water-based polyurethane, such as Deft
- Paper towels

TOOLS

- Band saw with blade: ¼" (6mm) wide
- Knives: carving, detail
- V-tools, 45°: ⅛" (3mm), ¼" (6mm)
- V-tool, 90°: ½" (13mm)
- #9 gouges: ¼" (6mm), ⅜" (10mm)
- Paintbrush
- Hair dryer (optional)

The author used these products for the project. Substitute your choice of brands, tools, and materials as desired.

MAKING A Mummy

That's a wrap! Carve this mesmerizing guy in just 12 steps

Think mummies are just for documentaries and history books? Tut-tut! It's clear you haven't met my friend Ralph. Ralph has just awoken from a long slumber and can't wait to explore the delights this new millennium has in store for him. Here we see Ralph just after learning that bandages now come in magenta and chartreuse—and he's making a beeline for the nearest pharmacy.

Getting Started

Cut your blank vertically in half from corner to corner; use a band saw. This will result in two triangles, one of which you can save for a future project. Photocopy the pattern, cut it out, and fold down the centerline. Trace the pattern (including the small diamond in front) onto one of the blanks, making sure the grain runs vertically from head to chest. (This gives more support to delicate areas.) Cut around the perimeter of the pattern with a band saw; I use a ¼" (6mm)-wide blade with 6 teeth-per-inch (TPI). If you don't have a band saw, you can use a coping saw or scroll saw. Save the paper pattern for future use.

Make sure all your tools are sharp, and periodically stretch your hands and wrists while carving.

ROUGHING OUT

1 **Cut the small triangle you just drew.** Use a knife.

2 **Draw the exposed facial area around the reference line you just cut.** Adjust the shape to fit as large an opening as you want.

3 **Cut downward to clear out the facial area.** Use the knife. Cut in across the bottom to remove the wood.

4 **Establish the basic shape.** Remove any sharp corners, flat spots, and saw marks with the knife.

5 **Taper the chin and neck.** Cut down under the chin into the neck area. This may take several cuts, as you want to create some shadows and depth. Remove the chips in the chest area with upward cuts. Then round the neck.

6 **Reestablish any definition you lost in the facial area while rounding.** Use the knife.

ADDING DETAILS

7 **Deepen the facial area.** Use a ¼" (6mm) 45° V-tool. Carve the top arc upward by laying the tool on its side. Carve the bottom line downward. By using the V-tool like a chisel, you create layers in the wood without having to go back with a knife. (See tip on page 5.)

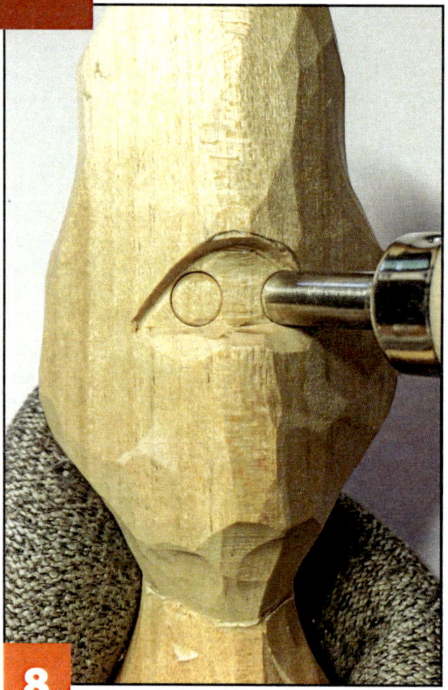

8 **Establish the eye position.** Use a ¼" (6mm) round punch to create two indentations at an equal distance from the center. Make sure they are even, as changing them later will be difficult without having to remove a lot of wood.

9 **Draw in the bandages with a gel pen.** (I find, when drawing too many reference lines with a pencil, that the graphite gets messy.) Notice how the pieces overlap, creating the opening for the eyes. Hold the body as you draw the lines on the head.

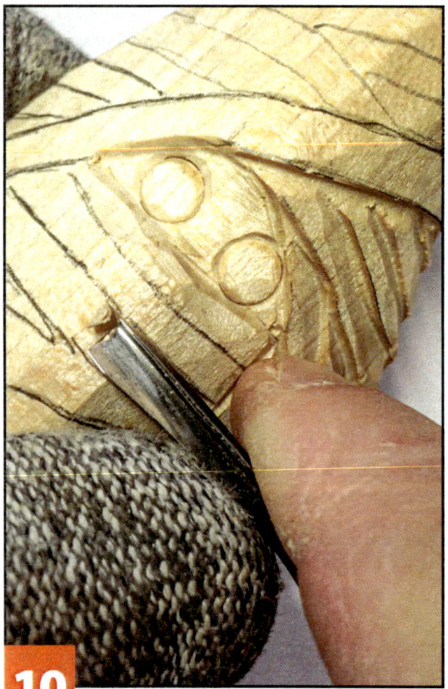

10 **Turn a ¼" (6mm) 45° V-tool on its side.** Then carve along the bottom of each line, with the point of the V angled slightly upward. This will create the impression that each section of the bandage overlaps the one under it.

11 **Cut out a small chip wherever the lines cross over each other.** Use the knife, as the V-tool won't be able to reach these areas effectively.

12 **Finish carving the bandages.** Add some areas where the wrap hangs down in order to break up all the horizontal lines. Clean up all remaining chips and fuzzies with the knife.

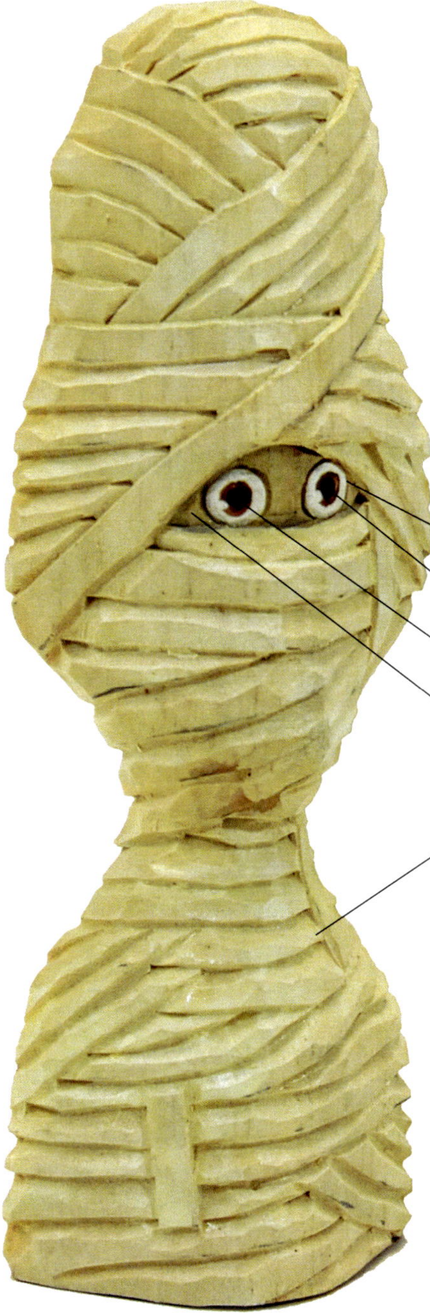

Paint List

White in eyes: unthinned white

Iris: unthinned nutmeg brown

Pupil: unthinned black

Face: 1 drop grey, 1 drop water

Bandages: 2 drops satin cream, 2 drops water

Acrylic paints: Plaid Apple Barrel

Painting and Finishing

Paint the eyes, skin, and bandages. If desired, use a hair dryer between colors to speed up the drying time. Add the irises, pupils, and shine to the eyes.

After everything is dry, brush on boiled linseed oil, which will give the bandages an aged look. Pat dry with clean paper towels, and let it dry again for three to four days. Finish as desired; I brushed on a water-based polyurethane.

Mummy Patterns

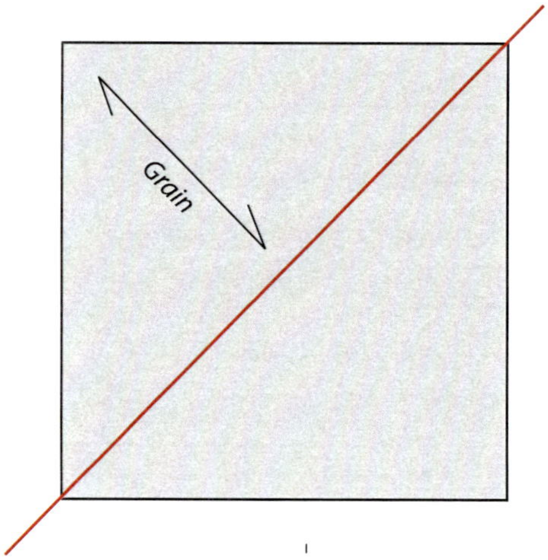

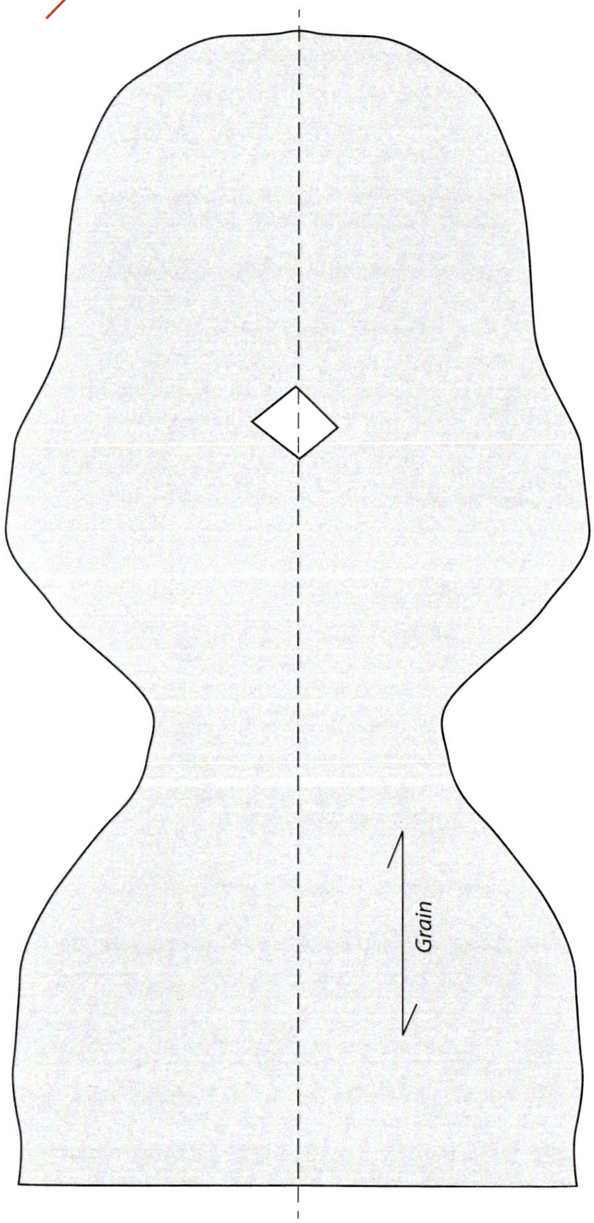

materials & **tools**

MATERIALS

- Basswood, 2" (5.1cm) square: 6" (15.2cm), cut vertically in half
- Pencil
- Gel pen
- Acrylic paints, such as Plaid Apple Barrel: black, grey, nutmeg brown, satin cream, white
- Boiled linseed oil
- Water-based polyurethane, such as Deft
- Paper towels

TOOLS

- Band saw with blade: ¼" (6mm) wide
- Carving knife
- V-tool, 45°: ¼" (6mm)
- Round punch: ¼" (6mm)
- Paintbrush
- Hair dryer (optional)

The author used these products for the project. Substitute your choice of brands, tools, and materials as desired.

Friendly Frank

This blue-eyed hunk will have you in stitches

We often envision Frankenstein's monster as someone scary, but in Mary Shelley's original story, he's a more complex figure. The gentleness and emotional intelligence he starts with actually make his descent into villainy all the more tragic at the end. You can portray your version of Frank in a number of ways, but I chose to give mine a friendly face.

Getting Started

Cut your blank vertically in half from corner to corner; use a band saw. This will result in two triangles, one of which you can save for a future project. Photocopy the pattern, cut it out, and fold down the centerline. Trace the pattern (including the small diamonds in front) onto one of the blanks, making sure the grain runs vertically from head to chest. (This gives more support to delicate areas, such as the nose.) Cut around the perimeter of the pattern with a band saw; I use a ¼" (6mm)-wide blade with 6 teeth-per-inch (TPI). If you don't have a band saw, you can use a coping saw or scroll saw. Save the paper pattern for future use.

Make sure all your tools are sharp, and periodically stretch your hands and wrists while carving.

ROUGHING OUT

1 **Remove the triangles in the center of the blank.** Use a regular carving knife.

2 **Cut deeper into the nose and the valley where the eyes are.** Use the knife to make a stop cut, and then carve up to the cut. This separates the nose from the face.

3 **Draw the hair, bottom of chin, neck, and ears.** Use a pencil. Then follow the lines with a ½" (13mm) 90° V-tool. Do not cut straight into the wood; lay the V-tool on its side and use it like a chisel. This helps to establish layers in the carving. (See tip on page 5.)

4 **Lower and shape the forehead.** Use a ½" (13mm) #9 gouge.

5 **Open up the eye sockets.** Use a ¼" (6mm) #9 gouge. Be sure not to cut through the bridge of the nose.

6 **Draw the ears and smile lines.** Then follow the smile lines with a ¼" (6mm) 45° V-tool. Turn the V-tool outward away from the nose; DO NOT cut toward the center of the nose on either side. This will erase any smooth transitions from nose to cheeks, making the nose look glued on.

ADDING DETAILS

7 **Shape the ears and nose.** Use the knife to round the tops of the ears. Cut a triangle on either side of the nose to further establish its shape. To do so, follow these steps: A) Cut slightly away from the nose in a downward cut under the nostril area. This angle will give his nose a round, button look. B) Cut into the smile line created earlier with the V-tool. C) Make a relief cut, creating a triangle on either side of the face.

8 **Round the hair, forehead, nose, chin, and shirt.** Use the knife. Cut the bolts into a roughly octagonal shape.

9 **Add detail to the mouth, ears, bolts, and shirt collar.** Use the ¼" (6mm) 45° V-tool. Then carve the upper eyelids and eye outline with the same tool. The upper eyelid is cut upward toward the brow, and the lower lid is cut downward toward the cheek. Avoid cutting straight into the eye at all times.

10 **Shape the eyes.** Use a detail knife. As in Step 9, all the cuts above the eye are made upward and those below are downward. Cut a triangle in each corner, removing the cut toward the center of the eye instead of straight in.

11 **Cut the nose holes.** Use the ¼" (6mm) #9 gouge upside down. Make these cuts straight into the nose, and remove the chip with the detail knife. Then draw the forehead scar and follow your lines with the ¼" (6mm) 45° V-tool. I gave him a straight cut, but you can give him some nastier scars if desired.

12 **Hollow the centers of the ears slightly.** Use a ¾" (19mm) #7 gouge. Make sure not to carve away the existing details in the process of adding these new ones.

13 **Break up the hairline.** Use the ½" (13mm) 90° V-tool upside down to cut in toward the forehead. Remove the chips with your knife of choice.

14 **Remove all pencil lines, fuzzies, high spots, and loose chips.** Make all finishing touches with the carving knife.

Paint Notes

Hair: 3 drops black (1), 2 drops water

Scar: unthinned red (1)

Flesh: 3 drops clover (2), 2 drops water

White in eyes: unthinned white (1)

Irises: unthinned blue bonnet (1)

Pupils: unthinned black (1)

Neck bolts: unthinned shimmering silver (3)

Clothing: 1 drop light grey (1), 1 drop water

1 Plaid Apple Barrel
2 Folk Art
3 Deco Art Metallics

Painting and Finishing

Paint the eyes, skin, and clothing. If desired, use a hair dryer between colors to speed up the drying time. Add the hair, irises, pupils, and shine to the eyes. Then add the scar and neck bolts.

After everything is dry, brush on boiled linseed oil, pat dry with clean paper towels, and let it dry again for three to four days. Finish as desired; I brushed on a water-based polyurethane.

Frankenstein Patterns

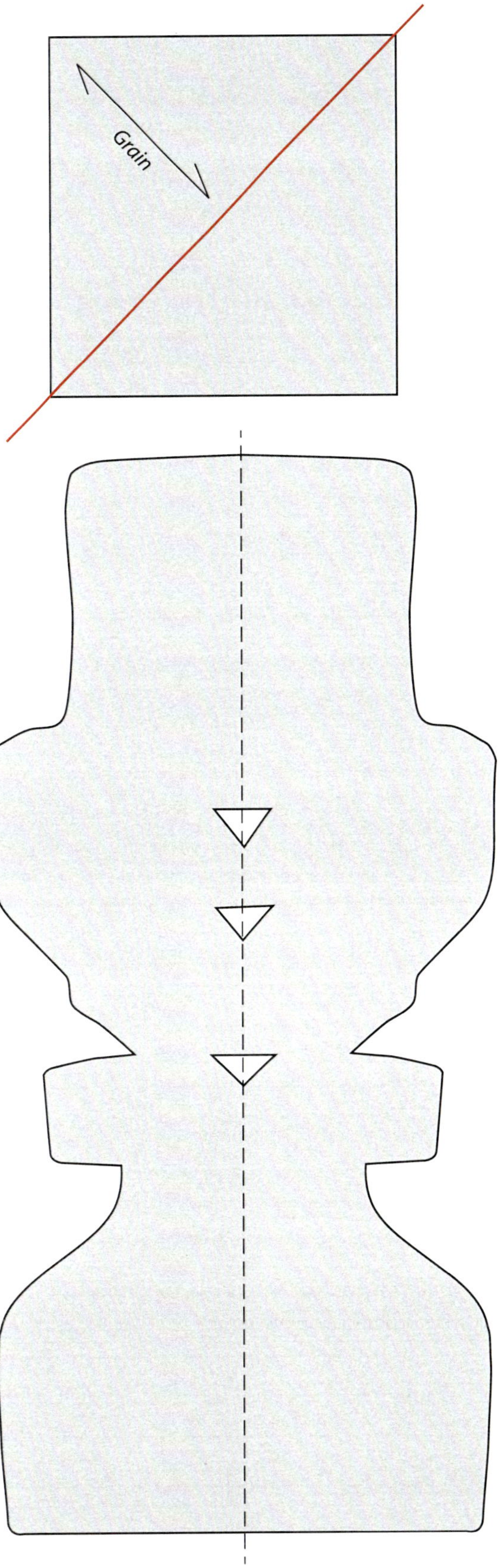

materials & **tools**

MATERIALS

- Basswood, 2" (5.1cm) square: 6" (15.2cm), cut vertically in half
- Pencil
- Acrylic paints, such as Plaid Apple Barrel: black, blue bonnet, light grey, red, white; such as Folk Art: clover; such as Deco Art Metallics: shimmering silver
- Boiled linseed oil
- Water-based polyurethane, such as Deft
- Paper towels

TOOLS

- Band saw with blade: ¼" (6mm) wide
- Carving knife
- V-tool, 45°: ¼" (6mm)
- V-tool, 90°: ½" (13mm)
- #7 gouge: ¾" (19mm)
- #9 gouge: ½" (13mm)
- Paintbrush
- Hair dryer (optional)

The author used these products for the project. Substitute your choice of brands, tools, and materials as desired.

Dedication

I want to extend my deepest thanks to everyone along the way who told me to keep carving and never give up. This book is dedicated to my loving wife, Melissa, for always supporting me throughout the endless woodchips—and to my daughter and son for always being there to help make the funny funnier.

Dwayne Gosnell lives in Hickory, N.C., and works in law enforcement. Carving gives him a break from his job, which is high-stress but allows him to view some pretty unique incidents, which often find their way into his caricatures. Dwayne started carving in 2006 and has been addicted ever since.